This book is designed for children in grades 2 through 6, to help track their training actions, and record accomplishments.

PUPPY TRAINING TRACKER

Kids

Bibliografische Information der Deutschen Nationalbibliothek:
Die Deutsche Nationalbibliothek verzeichnet diese Publikation in der Deutschen Nationalbibliografie; detaillierte bibliografische Daten sind im Internet über http://dnb.dnb.de abrufbar.

Herstellung und Verlag: BoD – Books on Demand, Norderstedt
ISBN: 978-3-7578-2912-4

THIS BOOK BELONGS TO:

TO THE FAMILY

Congratulations on your new family member! Growing up with a dog is a wonderful thing for children. Your child not only learns how to interact with a dog properly and to take responsibility, but also gains a lifelong companion.

However, a dog is neither a nanny nor a toy! It is an additional family member that requires care and education, for which you are responsible.

You must constantly supervise them. After a while, you can stay in the background, but need to be attentive and ready to intervene. Prepare for the extra steps required to teach your children how to handle the dog.

Initially, you will focus on teaching the puppy its name, feeding and relieving habits. The eventual goal for the first few weeks is to create a healthy relationship which will develop into a strong bond between you and your puppy (approx. around weeks 14 to 16).

As you get to know each other, you start to socialize your puppy in your own home, yard, and around the house followed by everything this world has to offer. Day-to-day situations must be mastered in puppyhood to expect a high level of security in adulthood.

- If you isolate your puppy from the environment, *lack of imprinting* occurs.
- If you scold your puppy, because it came too slowly, it experiences *negative imprinting.*
- Inappropriate limiting or influencing results in *misimprinting.*

During the first months it is important to pay special attention to social communication. Both, negative and positive influences, affect social (in)stability – forever! Try not to be hectic or even hysteric. Frequent, unprovoked physical threats, and loud scolding unsettle the puppy just as much as constant talking your puppy's ear off.

You have to give a lot of praise and confirmation for desired behaviors, ignore minor mischiefs, and clearly negate unwanted behaviors.

In conflict situations you need to protect, and show your puppy that it can feel save with you, by you being self-confident. Supposedly reassuring “don't be afraid” or petting in scary situations should be avoided, because it reinforces the feeling of fear.

Also with your spoken language, you convey important mood signals to the puppy. Thus, in addition to your body language, your voice is also a tool to motivate, confirm, interrupt and discourage puppies.

I wish you wonderful moments with your puppy,

Birgit

STRUCTURE OF THIS MANUAL

Core addresses each action. **Learning goal** regards both, you and your puppy. Following this, the **materials** or **resources** needed for the action are listed, along with the point in time – **PIT**, and your puppy's age at which they can be practiced.

Core lists the focus of the respective action. They pertain to your puppy.

Learning goal puppy: The intended learning goal related to the puppy through the action is specified.

Learning goal kid: The intended learning goal aimed at you through the action is specified.

Material: Minimal materials are required. They should be easily transferable and integrable into your daily life without much effort.

Reinforcement, praise and reward: This generally means anything that rewards your puppy – regardless of whether it's cuddling, a social play, or food. Sometimes, a specific reward such as a treat is mentioned. In such cases, it is assumed that this reward is the most suitable for the given task.

Less calm puppies need your "you can do it" **reinforcement**. Luring with treats into a sit, for example, is not good. Social attention, a **praising** voice, and cuddles represent more valuable rewards for the vast majority of puppies than food rewards.

Please note that highly motivated, lively puppies should be rewarded with regular dry food or gentle ear-tip massages and **praised** with a calming voice.

PIT: The time indications are rules of thumb. It must always be decided on a case-by-case basis in which time intervals your puppy should learn. With a highly motivated, puppy, you may start earlier and go ahead faster. If your puppy is resistant and calm, wait a couple of days before moving ahead.

"DO YOUR BUSINESS"

Core: Fulfill natural needs, calmness

Goal Puppy: To relieve only on natural ground, e.g., grass, gravel and eventually on command.

Goal Kid: To know the importance of regularly carrying the puppy outside, and **recognizes** when the puppy needs to be brought outside.

Material: Collar and Leash (optional)

PIT: Immediately

Puppies are physically not capable of going long periods without being relieved. It may take several weeks for a puppy to control its bladder and bowels for more than a few hours at a time (that is why babies wear diapers).

Don't rush! Your puppy needs to feel relaxed. Give your puppy a little time to just wander and sniff out its surroundings even when it rains (like some humans reading the newspaper on the toilet).

Times you need to carry your puppy outside:

- first thing in the morning
- after every meal
- after every drink
- after every play/training
- and last thing in the evening
- **when realizing excited sniffing out the floor**
- **when moving in a circle**
- **when whining in front of the door**

Carry your puppy to the designated washroom area and wait patiently. While relieving, praise it with your chosen command, e.g., "good business". You repeat this every time you bring the puppy to the washroom. By carrying your puppy, you decrease the possibility of accidents inside the house.

The key to success is consistency, patience, and supervision. Since puppies vary in their learning ability and dog owners vary in their teaching ability, there is no set rule for the duration of the training period.

Your puppy does not understand "just give me a second". If you are not fast enough the accident will happen because your puppy's body is not programmed to hold as long as you need to put on your shoes. Don't blame the puppy if an accident happened, it is your accident, not the puppy's. Immediate picking-up and carrying outside to the washroom is still required. Disinfect the spot thoroughly and be faster the next time.

Do not use dog pads. Once established inside, your dog will not differentiate between them and rugs, and only will go outside to have fun, but not for relieving.

If you don't have a garden: Put on the collar and leash, carry your puppy outside the house up to natural ground. Put it down, hold the leash, and wait patiently. While relieving, praise it with your chosen command, e.g., "good business".

"BE CALM"

Core: Relationship, Calmness and Patience

Goal Puppy: The puppy knows physical contact as a pleasant moment. It finds calmness in exciting situations.
Goal Kid: To establish physical contact with the puppy as a conscious action. To recognize when the puppy settles.

Material: -

PIT: Immediately at home, few weeks later in public

The ability to stay calm or to calm oneself down is advantageous in many everyday situations. Additionally, through this activity, the child can become more attuned to the effects of positive physical contact on the puppy and what type of physical contact the puppy finds pleasant. Many dog owners, for instance, pat their dog's head without realizing that the dog doesn't actually like it.

This activity works best when the puppy is already calm/tired. You stroke your puppy with slow movements until it displays clear signs of relaxation. These can include: Slow movements, reduced body tension, sitting down, lying down, lowering of the gaze, lowering of the head, blinking, slowing down of breathing, or deep exhalation.

When these signs become noticeable, you speak slowly and in a calming voice, saying "be calm". Due to classic conditioning, the words "be calm" can become a cue. For this, you should say it as often as possible in situations where the puppy is calm.

The time it takes for the association to be established depends on the specific type of puppy and the frequency of practice. If you have the opportunity to perform the activity with the puppy every evening, "be calm" can be used as a cue to calm the puppy in slightly exciting situations after a few weeks.

After a few weeks, parents and kid can train the puppy to "be calm" in public. If the puppy has already had fun and exercise, they can sit on a bench with a sufficient distance from other dogs and environmental stressors and try to perform the same activity as at home.

"BITE INHIBITION"

Core: Social behaviour, perception, and awareness

Goal Puppy: The puppy learns that tooth contact with a human skin is not desired.

Goal Kid: The kid learns to set boundaries.

Resource: Parents

PIT: Immediately

Bite inhibition refers to the puppy's ability to control the force of their bite, and to a person's ability to control the puppy's biting impulses.

Bite inhibition begins to solidify within the natural family among siblings and also towards the mother, father, and other adult dogs within the unit. It is also a responsibility of the breeder to start with this training. This is one of the reasons why it's important to leave the puppy with the breeder until the 12th week, as bite inhibition is not fully developed before that.

The puppy receives negative feedback when it uses its teeth; an outraged 'Hey!'. If that doesn't work, the game is interrupted by both, the child and the parent standing up. If the puppy continues regardless, the game is completely stopped, and the child and parent briefly go to another room. If the puppy follows, snapping at their legs, become reprimanded; parent leans over him saying 'Stop that!' or stomp on the ground, kid needs to be on the same page.

The puppy learns that the game ends as soon as it uses its teeth. However, since it wants to continue playing, it stops the behavior – and the game can continue.

Consistency is key; any tooth contact must be marked as undesirable.

"OFF YOU GO"

Core: Attention, communication, patience

Goal Puppy: The puppy learns to pay attention, to stay with the kid, and to only leave when allowed by OFF YOU GO.

Goal Kid: The kid learns to stay consistent by asking for the puppy's attention, even if there are distractions.

Material: Collar, leash, treat/dry food.

PIT: Immediately inside the house/garden, when established outside.

This is one of the most important tasks and is closely associated with "HERE".

The puppy is leashed inside the house and led into the garden. The child now attempts to get the puppy's attention. As soon as the puppy looks at the child, the carabiner is snapped without releasing it. If the puppy stays with the child for one second without changing its previously adopted position, the puppy receives praise and a reward.

In the next attempt, the child waits for two seconds, then three seconds in the following one. In the next step, the child waits three seconds again, then releases the carabiner if the puppy still remains with the child for one second. The child happily and energetically says, 'off you go,' and moves in the direction the puppy is facing, away from the puppy. If the puppy follows the child, it receives a reward. If the puppy goes elsewhere, that's also okay, because 'off you go' means the puppy can do whatever it wants.

The next day, the child starts with three seconds and increases it to ten seconds. If the puppy leaves its adopted position at any point, the child signals disappointment: 'Oh, too bad,' lowering the head, letting it hang, and turning away from the puppy.

Then another attempt follows, but the time span is reduced again. If the exercise works, a distraction is introduced, such as placing the favorite toy, visible to the puppy by Mom, going back to five seconds and gradually increase it to ten seconds again.

If this exercise works, the toy is no longer placed by Mom but is thrown by the child. This activates the hunting behavior, and we have to go back to five seconds.

This exercise is needed in everyday situations during walks.

"PUPPY, HERE"

Core: Attention, communication, bonding

Goal Puppy: The puppy learns to come when called.

Goal Kid: The kid learns to pay attention to the puppy's behaviour and to take over leadership.

Material: Collar, leash, high value food, such as Mozzarella, liver paste

PIT: Immediately inside the house/garden, when established outside

This is one of the most important tasks and is closely associated with "OFF YOU GO".

Some puppies are not addressable as soon as they are immersed in the world of scents. Therefore, this command needs to be trained at home first. Increase the distance: kitchen corner to kitchen corner, kitchen to living room, kitchen to bed room, kitchen to garden. All of the above vice versa. Garden corner to garden corner, increase by adding distractions, etc.

- ♫ Puppy ♫ here ♫ – a high-pitched singing voice or baby voice increases puppy's attention
- As soon as the puppy looks, the kid kneels down
- While the pup is coming, the kid makes a happy face
- As soon as the pup arrived, the kid praises "good here".
- While praising, the kid gives tiny squares of high value food, piece by piece or liver paste that the puppy needs to suck out of the tube.
- The kid stands up: "OFF YOU GO".
- To be repeated every 15 meters, whether the pup is in front or behind

Your body language should always be open and friendly, your face happy, your posture small – without bending forward.

Once the puppy starts to connect the word „here" with the action of running to you, you start to change walking directions without telling or you hide behind a bush. As soon as the pup arrives, you throw a big food party.

You can also capture wanted behavior: Every time the pup stops and looks to you, put on a big smile or say "hello puppy". If your puppy comes to you without being asked to do so, praise „good here" with a big smile but without a reward, because you did not ask for the task.

"PUPPY, WITH ME"

Core: Attention, communication, bonding

Goal Puppy: The puppy learns to stick as close as possible to the leading leg without pulling on leash and zig zagging.

Goals Kid: The kid learns to not let the puppy pull, to not catch up with the pup when in front, to not wait for the puppy when behind and to focus on the pup.
Material: Collar, leash, treats.

PIT: Immediately inside the house/garden, when established in public.

Another fundamental and indispensable command is "WITH ME". You need it in pedestrian areas, on busy roads, in train stations and other dangerous places.

Once you said „WITH ME", the puppy is not allowed to sniff, to pee, to run ahead nor to stay behind.

Start at home. You decide on what side you want to lead your puppy. On that side you have a leading leg and a leading hand. The leash is in your leading hand, and treats are in your opposite hand. Your reward with the opposite hand.

	What you say	What you do
When your puppy is next to your leading leg, and you both face the same direction	„Puppy, with me!"	Watch your puppy
When your puppy looks at you	„Good, with me."	Give a treat next to your leading knee, stand up.
	„Puppy, with me!"	Make one step with your leading leg.
When your puppy follows	„Good, with me."	Give a treat next to your leading knee, stand up.

Repeat a couple of times, then use the "OFF YOU GO", to give your puppy a break. Let it sniff or send it away by throwing a treat.

Start all over, eventually you make three steps, then five, seven, etc. If at one point the puppy gets distracted and pulls, you immediately stop moving, **and get the pup back to you. Do not go where it is**. Always move naturally, do not lure with the treat in front of the pup's nose.

"LEAVE IT / DROP IT"

Core: Attention, communication, safe keeping

Goal Puppy: The puppy learns not to touch / drop something.

Goal Kid: The kid learns to read the pup, and to realize when the puppy is about to pick something up.

Material: Dry food, box, high value food.

PIT: Immediately inside the house

It is always better to avoid unwanted behavior than to interrupt it. Not least because this could save your pups' life someday.

To teach „leave it" you need regular treats in a box, for your puppy to smell but not to reach, and high value food.

Leave the puppy in one room. Put the box with the treats in the middle of a second room, then get your puppy inside the room with the box. As soon as your puppy zeroes into the scent source, you give a very harsh and threatening vocal „LEAVE IT!". Your puppy will startle and look at you, like what did I do wrong?

That is the moment you immediately put on your smiling party face, praise happily „good leave it" and reward with the high value food.

Repeat the exercise the following day, for a couple of days. Exchange the dry food for high value food, and give it a couple of repetitions. Do it outside with a couple of repetitions, then built it into your daily strolls.

Harder to train is the „DROP IT". The timing and your social competence are critical. If your puppy already has something in the mouth, calmly go to it and take it away with „DROP IT!". If it does not want to give the object, press lightly with one hand from above against the muzzle until the puppy opens the mouth. Calmly take the object out of the mouth praising „good drop it" and reward with a high value treat.

The calmer you remain, the greater the chance that it will not choke down the object or try to run away with it.

PUPPY TRAINING

I START ON

AND DO IT ON

MON	TUE	WED	THU	FRI	SAT	SUN
☐	☐	☐	☐	☐	☐	☐
TIME	TIME	TIME	TIME	TIME	TIME	TIME

IN / AT

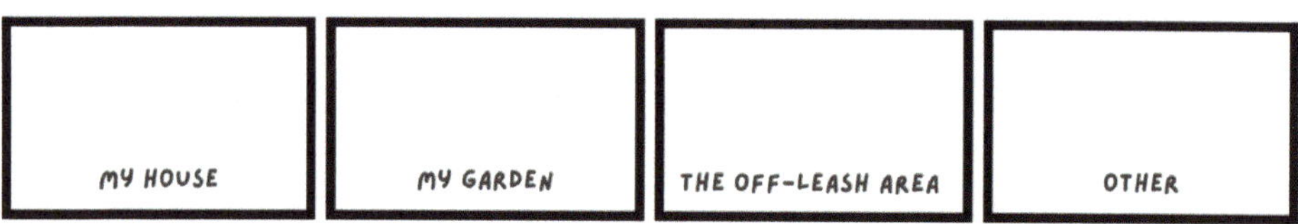

MATERIAL

SKILLS MY PUPPY NEEDS TO LEARN

SKILLS I WANT TO LEARN

MY ACTION SERVES THIS GOAL

WHAT I NEED TO DO ACCORDING TO PAGE __

STEP 1

STEP 2

STEP 3

WHO COULD HELP?

MY ACTION SERVES THIS GOAL

WHAT I NEED TO DO ACCORDING TO PAGE __

STEP 1

STEP 2

STEP 3

WHO COULD HELP?

MY ACTION SERVES THIS GOAL

WHAT I NEED TO DO ACCORDING TO PAGE __

STEP 1

STEP 2

STEP 3

WHO COULD HELP?

MY ACTION SERVES THIS GOAL

WHAT I NEED TO DO ACCORDING TO PAGE __

STEP 1

STEP 2

STEP 3

WHO COULD HELP?

MY ACTION SERVES THIS GOAL

WHAT I NEED TO DO ACCORDING TO PAGE __

STEP 1

STEP 2

STEP 3

WHO COULD HELP?

MY ACTION SERVES THIS GOAL

WHAT I NEED TO DO ACCORDING TO PAGE __

STEP 1

STEP 2

STEP 3

WHO COULD HELP?

MY ACTION SERVES THIS GOAL

WHAT I NEED TO DO ACCORDING TO PAGE __

STEP 1

STEP 2

STEP 3

WHO COULD HELP?

MY ACTION SERVES THIS GOAL

WHAT I NEED TO DO ACCORDING TO PAGE __

STEP 1

STEP 2

STEP 3

WHO COULD HELP?

PUPPY TRAINING IS FUN

WEEK OF ____________ WAS

WHAT WE PRACTICED

What I learned	What my puppy learned

KEEP PRACTICING / NEXT STEPS

-
-
-
-
-
-
-

WEEK OF ____________ WAS

WHAT WE PRACTICED

What I learned	What my puppy learned

KEEP PRACTICING / NEXT STEPS

-
-
-
-
-
-
-

WEEK OF ____________ WAS

WHAT WE PRACTICED

What I learned

What my puppy learned

KEEP PRACTICING / NEXT STEPS

•
•
•
•
•
•
•

SKILL TRACKER

Skill	Insert time span or no. of accomplishments or a ✓						

WEEK OF ____________ WAS

WHAT WE PRACTICED

What I learned

What my puppy learned

KEEP PRACTICING / NEXT STEPS

-
-
-
-
-
-
-

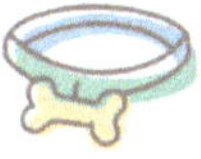 PUPPY TRAINING IS FUN

WEEK OF ____________ WAS

WHAT WE PRACTICED

What I learned	What my puppy learned

KEEP PRACTICING / NEXT STEPS

-
-
-
-
-
-
-

PUPPY TRAINING IS FUN

WEEK OF ____________ WAS

WHAT WE PRACTICED

What I learned	What my puppy learned

KEEP PRACTICING / NEXT STEPS

-
-
-
-
-
-
-

SKILL TRACKER

Skill

Insert time span or no. of accomplishments or a ✓

WEEK OF ____________ WAS

WHAT WE PRACTICED

What I learned	What my puppy learned

KEEP PRACTICING / NEXT STEPS

-
-
-
-
-
-
-

PUPPY TRAINING IS FUN

WEEK OF ____________ WAS

WHAT WE PRACTICED

What I learned

What my puppy learned

KEEP PRACTICING / NEXT STEPS

-
-
-
-
-
-
-

WEEK OF ____________ WAS

WHAT WE PRACTICED

What I learned

What my puppy learned

KEEP PRACTICING / NEXT STEPS

-
-
-
-
-
-
-

SKILL TRACKER

Skill

Insert time span or no. of accomplishments or a ✓

WEEK OF ____________ WAS

WHAT WE PRACTICED

What I learned	What my puppy learned

KEEP PRACTICING / NEXT STEPS

-
-
-
-
-
-
-

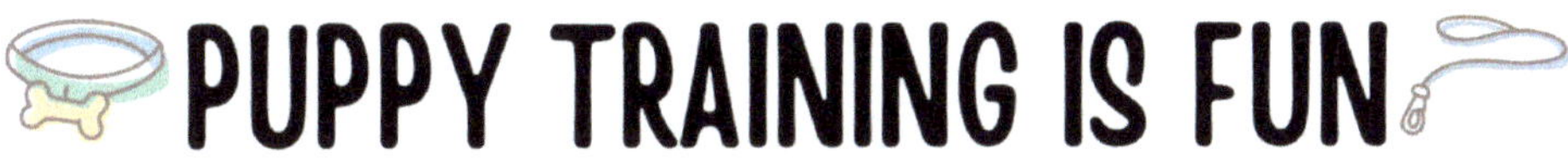

WEEK OF ____________ WAS

WHAT WE PRACTICED

What I learned	What my puppy learned

KEEP PRACTICING / NEXT STEPS

-
-
-
-
-
-
-

WEEK OF ____________ WAS

WHAT WE PRACTICED

What I learned	What my puppy learned

KEEP PRACTICING / NEXT STEPS

-
-
-
-
-
-
-

SKILL TRACKER

Skill

Insert time span or no. of accomplishments or a ✓